LIFE SINKS OR SOARS
– THE CHOICE IS YOURS

RAEL KALLEY

1-888-929-0343

email: Ididit@strategicpathways.net

Library and Archives Canada
Cataloguing in Publication

Kalley, Rael
Life sinks or soars – the choice is yours – First Edition

ISBN 978-0-9865521-0-6

© 2010 by Rael Kalley
ISBN 978-0-9865521-0-6

Publisher:
Strategic Pathways

Design and Production:
Mark Woodbeck, WaiteWoodbeck Creative Garage, Calgary, Alberta

Project Management:
Debbie Elicksen, Freelance Communications, Calgary, Alberta

Life sinks or soars – the choice is yours – First Edition

Printed and bound in Canada

Copyright 2010

Prologue:

Thursday March 12

"Hello. This is Hugh." Just hearing his deep baritone answer the phone with the same greeting he has used for as long as I've known him caused me to start feeling better right away.

Hugh and I have had a friendship that dates back to our teens so many, many years ago.

We were both thirteen when fate caused our two paths to collide. Hugh happened to walk into the school gym just as Brian, David and Gary, the fearsome trio whose schoolyard reign of terror caused many an anxious moment, were about to reposition certain body parts of mine because I had the audacity to refuse their demands to hand over my lunch.

Even at that young age Hugh exhibited an uncanny ability to understand human psychology. He rushed over to my side, immediately identified Brian as the gang leader, pushed him to the ground and, in a chillingly menacing voice that I vividly remember to this day, told David and Gary what their fate would be if they came one step closer.

As is the case with all bullies, when challenged, they turned and fled with Brian picking himself up off the ground and stumbling after them.

Our friendship began in that moment and has lasted to this day.

We were an improbable pair. Hugh was, and still is, tall, good looking and athletic. I am, um, none of the above and yet from that unlikely beginning we became inseparable.

Throughout high school and into early adulthood we did everything together. Hugh's large circle of friends became my friends and for the first time in my life I felt accepted.

Suddenly I found myself included in party invitations, burger outings, dates, poker, movies, sport and all other events befitting members of the inner circle.

We became each others sounding boards for all matters. We sought each others advice and input on dating, schoolwork, acne and every other topic of teenage importance.

1

I often wondered why we were friends. We were so different. He was so accomplished and I always felt we were unequal's. He seemed to effortlessly excel in everything he did; school, sports, music, attracting friends. I, on the other hand, seemed capable only of mediocrity. I achieved average results in most of those things and, as a wise person once said, "average simply means you are the best of the worst or the worst of the best."

As the years passed and we transitioned through adolescence, early adulthood, marriage(s), careers, families and into the present day of middle age the bonds of our friendship grew stronger despite long gaps in contact as our lives took us in different directions and the sheer busyness of life frequently nudged the friendship out of immediate focus.

We both knew that despite these interruptions in continuity, we were always there for each other, in an instant, if needed.

We were often out of contact for a year or more and yet each time we did reconnect it was like a magical reunion that caused the time gaps to evaporate as if we had never spent a day apart. We just simply picked up where we had left off. We both knew the rarity of this type of relationship and, while we never discussed this, I'm sure Hugh felt as blessed as I do for the friendship that has transcended more than four decades.

As close as we were as friends in the similarities of our dreams and desires for our lives, we were as opposite as possible in what we accomplished in our lives.

By the time we were twenty-five Hugh had started a technology company and sold it to an investment fund for a gazillion dollars. I was struggling to pay my phone bill.

By thirty Hugh had been married to Brenda, his high school sweetheart, for seven years and they had produced a Hugh clone named Michael and a beautiful daughter, Jill. I was close to the end of my second marriage.

By forty Hugh had started and sold two additional companies and was semi-retired, consulting to businesses around the world and running the foundation he and Brenda had established to teach entrepreneurship to young adults. I was struggling through my third business, having shut one down and given the other to a person who was willing to assume the debt.

By fifty Hugh's life was a whirlwind of luxurious holidays, family functions, grandchildren, two best-selling management books and he was constantly feted as a guest lecturer at organizations all over the world. My business was barely paying its bills and there was always too much month left at the end of the money. For me a holiday was taking a day away from the office to catch up on repairs to the house.

Despite the disparity in our life accomplishments, our friendship had always remained strong. I was truly delighted by Hugh's successes and he was never judgmental of my failures. He had always told me that if I wanted his advice I need only ask and that he would never offer me any unsolicited advice.

True to his word he had listened intently each time I had explained my next grand plan and had always been there to offer comfort and encouragement when my grandiose ideas failed to reach my expectations.

We shared in each others joy. I was the best man at his wedding. He was the best man at all three of mine (he told me he owned a wash and wear tux that he had bought just for my weddings).

I am Michael's godfather and was in the waiting room at the hospital when Jill was born. I don't have children so he named all three of my dogs.

I attended the celebrations each time he sold a business. He was at the grand opening of each of mine.

We also shared in each others sorrows. He was a pall bearer when my parents passed away. I was with him when he identified his father's remains after he had been struck by a drunk driver.

He was there when I was diagnosed with a devastating, life threatening illness and his was the first face I saw when I opened my eyes after life-saving surgery.

And tragically, I was by his side, along with Michael and Jill, when, three years ago Brenda succumbed to the breast cancer she had fought so valiantly for six years.

A year later Hugh had packed his broken heart and moved to New York, where both Michael and Jill lived with their families. We have not spoken since then.

"Hi Hugh, it's Earl," I breathed into the phone. "It's great to hear your voice, how are you?"

"Earl? What a pleasant surprise. I've been thinking that I should call you. It's been so long. How are you?"

"I'm terrific," I lied. "I thought two years was long enough so I decided to check in on you. God knows if I'd waited for you to call I'd have died of old age."

Even in my fifties I still can't help being a smartass.

We spent ten minutes or so getting caught up on each others lives and then Hugh asked "So Earl, it's terrific hearing from you, I'm delighted you called. Now what's the real reason why you are calling?"

I wasn't surprised by the question. I have never been able to keep anything from him.

I took a deep breath, paused and slowly exhaled. "Hugh," I began, "I really need to talk to you.

"I am at a point in my life where I just don't know what to do. It seems my whole life has been a series of things blowing up in my face and no matter what I do I can't seem to break the cycle of never succeeding at anything in the long term."

"I know," he said. "I've been expecting this call for a long time. I've watched you struggle for so many years and I worry about you a lot. How bad is it?"

"I don't know if it's any worse than it has always been, it's just that it never seems to get better and my ability to deal with the never-ending stress is not what it used to be. I always used to believe that if I just hung in there things would get better but now I find myself anticipating the worst in everything I do. Frankly Hugh, I'm exhausted. I don't like the thoughts that keep going through my head, you know, the thoughts that keep telling me that it will never get better and that I would be better off dead."

"Earl," he interrupted, "are you saying what I think you're saying?"

"I'm not sure I know what I'm saying, Hugh. I feel that I have no control over my life and I seem to have lost all faith in my ability to do anything. My self confidence has nose-dived into the ground and I don't know if I have the strength to keep fighting, or if I even want to."

"Earl I know you won't believe this but I know exactly how you feel. And, I promise you, there is a way out. If you remember, a long time ago I promised you I would never offer advice unless you asked for it. Please tell me you're asking now."

"I am asking" I said, "I might even be begging."

"Well" Hugh interjected, "we promised each other years ago that we would always be there for each other and we always have. In the time of my greatest need, when Brenda died, you were there and you were my rock. Without you to lean on I don't think I would have survived those terrible days.

"Now it's my turn. I will be there in two days. I need you to book two rooms at a hotel and promise me you will move into one of those rooms for three days, with no outside interruptions, while we figure this out. Do we have a deal?"

"Sure," I replied feeling both hopeful that there may be a solution and guilty that Hugh was going to fly all the way here just to listen to my sad tale of woe.

I gave him the name of the hotel where we would meet, said goodbye and hung up.

Chapter 1

A few days later I checked into the hotel and waited for Hugh to arrive.

I knew Hugh would do everything in his power to help me but I wasn't sure that I believed anything could change or that I could find the energy within myself to keep going.

So I prepared a "Plan B."

For a long time sleep had seemed the only escape from the constant feelings of despair and uncertainty I had become accustomed to. Sleep seemed the only time when I didn't have to make the decisions I felt incapable of making, the only time when I didn't focus on all that was wrong in my life and the only time when that relentless knot of fear and worry would leave my stomach.

Sleep had come to mean freedom from anxiety for me and had become so desirable that I had decided that if for any reason I still felt as defeated after spending time with Hugh as I was feeling now, then going to sleep and not waking up would be the preferred way for me to permanently rid myself of all I could not face and to prepare for a peaceful eternity.

I had even written out a detailed "to do" list to ensure that nothing was forgotten and everything was performed in the planned sequence. I called it my "Checkout Check list."

I'm a funny guy.

To prepare for this possibility, I had done my research expertly. Google led me exactly to where I needed to go to acquire the pharmacological expertise necessary to successfully expedite my demise and using both legitimate and devious means I had stockpiled a sufficient quantity of products to guarantee satisfaction.

I had also visited the local liquor store and purchased enough booze to ensure that everything would go down smoothly and, remembering that "things go better with coke" I had acquired a substantial amount from the 'franchisee' who seemed to own the rights to the local neighborhood distribution center.

I placed all of this in a bag under the bed.

My exit material.

Did I mention the hotel was called Journey's End?

I'm a funny guy.

Chapter 2

Shortly after 6 o'clock the phone rang. It was Hugh calling to let me know he had just checked into his room. We arranged to meet in the lobby in an hour.

I found him pacing the lobby. One of the most annoying things about him is that he never seems to age. He looked tanned, fit and healthy, his thick mane as dark brown as always.

Damn.

I headed right over and we did one of those shoulder to shoulder guy-hug things. "You're looking great," he said, making no mention of the fact that there was at least thirty pounds more of me to look at than when we had last seen each other.

We exchanged niceties and decided to head out to a small bistro in the next block. Hugh, ever the wine connoisseur, ordered an expensive bottle of Chateau Something Pretentious. I'm a non-drinker and settled for a cola.

"Hugh," I started, "I just want to say how much I appreciate ..."

He interrupted me by shaking his head and holding up his hand in the universal stop position. "Usquequaque illic," he proclaimed, reciting the pledge we had sworn during that first year of our friendship.

Usquequaque illic.

I remembered the evening like it was yesterday. The frantic phone call from him "can you come to the hospital right now. I need you. My parents have been in an accident and they're in really bad shape..." The rest was lost to unintelligible crying. I said I would be there right away and went and told my mother what had happened.

She immediately turned off the oven and said "let's go." She drove me to the hospital with wanton disregard for speed limits. We parked the car and rushed inside.

Hugh was sitting next to a kindly looking police officer in the waiting room in Emergency. He looked lost and terrified. He looked up at Mom and me. He started to cry. So did I. He flew into my mothers arms his shoulders shaking uncontrollably as he tried to tell us what had happened.

In between gasping sobs the story came out. They were on their way out to dinner to celebrate Hugh's mother's birthday. As his father entered an intersection a small delivery van blew through the red light smashing into the front passenger door of their car forcing it into a street light on the opposite side of the street before rolling several times and coming to a stop several hundred feet from the point of impact.

Miraculously Hugh was only slightly shaken up but otherwise unhurt. His parents suffered serious injuries and were both rushed, unconscious, to hospital. The police officer had driven Hugh to the hospital and stayed with him until we arrived.

A nurse materialized from behind a door and informed us that both his parents had suffered severe, life threatening injuries and were in surgery. She would keep us informed.

Hugh has no siblings and his relatives all lived in other cities. For the moment we were his family and support system and for the next two days I did not leave his side. We took turns sitting at his mother's bedside and then at his father's, waiting, waiting, waiting.

My mother came by several times each day bringing us hot meals and fresh clothes. She knew I needed to be there and encouraged me to stay as long as necessary. She called our school and explained why we would both be absent for a while.

After two days we received the best news possible. Hugh's parents were out of danger. They would have full recoveries.

Hugh stayed with us for several weeks until his parents were released and Mom took meals to their house each day until they were back on their feet.

Several months later, now completely recovered, Hugh's parents took Mom and me out for dinner as a way of saying thank you and to celebrate their miraculous recoveries.

At some point in the evening Hugh's mother commented on how grateful she was that Hugh had a friend like me who was there for him, without question, when needed.

I pointed out that it was Hugh who, without thought for his own safety, had stood up to three older bullies to save me from a beating.

I'll never forget what happened next. Hugh looked at me and it was as if we could read each others mind. He picked up his steak knife and, using the sharp point at the end, stuck it into the tip of his right thumb, drawing a tiny bead of blood. I immediately did the same and we pressed our right thumbs together and, at exactly the same moment, chanted a phrase we had learned in Latin class that week. "Usquequaque illic" – always there.

No matter what.

"Look" Hugh suggested, snapping me back to the present. "Let's make tonight a fun night, a celebration of our many years of friendship. Let's pretend all is great with the world. Let's reminisce about the good old days, laugh and joke, tell each other great lies about all our wondrous exploits and all of this while we feast on decadent amounts of fattening food.

"Tomorrow we'll go to work and see if your sorry soul is even worth saving." He raised his glass to affirm this arrangement.

And celebrate we did. I cannot remember the last time I had laughed myself to tears. We went back to Day One and howled hysterically at the memories of Brian, David and Gary running for their lives. We recounted our teenage dating years and each conquest we recalled became more and more magnificent in the telling. Even, I suspect, the ones that had only taken place in our heads.

We giggled at the memories of the day we let the air out of each tire of the principal's car and recalled with glee the time we had "borrowed" an advance copy of a history exam by picking the lock on the teachers locker (even at fourteen Hugh had shown signs of the remarkable diversity of his skills) and sold sufficient copies to our classmates to finance a dinner "meeting" for our six closest friends that we held at the local burger joint.

We remembered fondly the cigar club we had formed in Hugh's bedroom when we were sixteen and vividly recalled our panicked response when his father had burst into the room having been alerted to our newest project by the pungent aroma wafting through the house. Apparently our belief that keeping his bedroom window wide open would provide sufficient ventilation to remove all evidence of wrongdoing had been misplaced.

We relived the night we went for a drive in Hugh's fathers new Jaguar conveniently forgetting that we had neither permission nor drivers licenses; how we were thirty minutes late for Hugh's wedding because I had left the rings at home and we had to go back to get them; the time Hugh called to tell me his car had been stolen from his home before realizing that he had taken a cab home from the bar the previous night and left the car at work.

And so many more. Each time Hugh told a story, I had a better one to follow.

Same with him.

I felt lighter and happier than at any time in recent memory and the more embellished our stories became the more relaxed and care-free I felt.

In between howls of uncontrollable laughter we gorged ourselves on vast quantities of exotic *cuisine* with unpronounceable names and out-of-this-world prices.

Finally, after midnight, with the restaurant long empty and the staff noisily vacuuming around us, Hugh paid the bill and we strolled back to the hotel all the while grinning like two errant choirboys.

"I have a few early morning calls to make," Hugh informed me as we entered the hotel. "Let's meet in your room at 9:30."

Goodnight.

Chapter 3

At 9:30am there was a gentle tap on the door. Hugh. He came into the room and sat down at the ubiquitous round table that seems to be a requisite piece of furniture in every hotel room on the planet.

"Well," he said, "let's get started. Why don't you tell me what's going on and let's see if we can understand why this is happening."

I poured coffee and began, "Hugh, today, for the first time in my life I am going to be honest. I am going to tell the truth about who I am to another person. It's a truth I have always hidden from you and have been hiding from the whole world for as long as I can remember. When you said you would fly over and spend some time with me that was when I realized that this is probably the best chance I will ever have to confront the truths that I have fought so hard to hide.

"I'm not doing this because you came when I called; I'm not doing this for you, my best friend, as much as I appreciate you as a true friend who has never once judged me harshly. No! I'm going to do this for me because I have finally realized that if I don't remove the shackles of delusion I have worn for so long, I will remain chained to the insecurities I have lived with all my life.

"So here goes.

"You know, I can't think of a time in my life when I have ever liked who I am. My earliest memories are of feelings of inadequacy, of not ever feeling that I was good enough; not smart enough to get good grades in school; not athletic enough make the football team; not good looking enough to get a date; not bright enough to go to college; not savvy enough to run a business; not committed enough to sustain a marriage; not ambitious enough to provide for a family, not, not, not, not, not.

"I have always had this feeling of imminent failure. Regardless of what I have done, regardless of how enthusiastically I have portrayed myself to be, regardless of how energized and motivated I have appeared to be on the outside, on the inside I have always doubted my abilities and have always had this feeling, this belief inside myself that whatever I began would ultimately fail.

"I have no memories of family togetherness. As a young child I remember my parents always fighting about money. I remember thinking that there was only a little bit of money in the whole world and we didn't have any of it.

"As they argued I thought that it was because of me that there wasn't enough money. I cost more than they had and I blamed myself for all the things our family didn't have.

"I do remember asking God to let me die in my sleep so my parents would have more money and I learned very young not to ask for anything because each time I did ask I was reminded that 'we're not made of money' and that 'money doesn't grow on trees.'

"I learned to be ashamed of who I was. When my parents came to drive me home after school I would ask them to park a few blocks away so that no-one would see how old and battered their car was.

"I didn't invite anyone over to play for the same reasons.

"And I learned to believe that that is the way life is. Some have, we don't.

"As I got older I became very self conscious about my looks. I was a pudgy kid and used to compare myself to all those tall, good looking guys at school. I got in the habit of starving myself. I used to skip breakfast and give my lunch to anyone who wanted it. I spent hours exercising in my room and no matter how hard I tried, even when I got in really good shape, I still felt like the fat kid who everyone made fun of behind his back.

"Then my parents divorced and my mother became a single mom back in the days before that phrase had even entered our lexicon.

"When you and I first became friends I couldn't believe my good luck and, for the first while, I suspected that our friendship was part of a conspiracy to humiliate me that would end with me being laughed out of the friendship.

"Even at school I didn't work very hard because I didn't believe it would matter. I wasn't going to have a chance to do much with my life anyway.

"You remember how you used to have to force me into asking girls out on dates. It wasn't because I didn't want to go out with them, as I kept telling you, it was because I was so convinced that they wouldn't want to go out with me and I didn't want the pain of rejection.

"And yes, you always convinced me to make the calls. I could never say no to you and so, thanks to you, we ended up having lots of fun dates.

"When I first started working I only looked for menial jobs because I didn't think I was worthy or capable of anything better and it wasn't until you started your first company that I began to think that maybe I could own a business too.

"When my first business didn't do very well I almost felt a sense of relief. It was like I had known this would happen, had expected it to happen and the sense of relief was confirmation that I wasn't good enough to have my own business.

"At my wedding I remember overhearing one of my mother's friends jokingly wonder out loud how long the marriage would last and thinking that my grandparent's marriage had failed, my parents were divorced so divorce was probably in my destiny. You know, continuing the family tradition.

"As you know that marriage lasted less than two years and I remember telling you of my feelings of relief when it ended.

"Hugh, I'm not going to take all day to go through each year of my life. I think you know what I'm saying. I just feel like I have had this cloud of unworthiness hovering over my head from the day I was born and I have lived up to my own expectations of failure and hardship with only intermittent periods of happiness.

"Right now I'm at the point where I have to start all over again. At a time in my life when my friends are beginning to retire and travel the world, I'm not sure I'll be able to keep my business going for another month and if I can't, I don't know if I have the energy or desire to try again. I keep asking myself 'what's the point of trying again? The results will just be the same.'

"And you know, Hugh, even if I decide to try one more time, I don't know what I would do or what I can do.

"I've always wanted you to see me as a worthy friend. I've always needed your respect and I've always wanted to believe that you saw me as an equal so I have never asked you for help. I've never asked what makes you so successful because I needed to believe that you believed I had the same abilities.

"I have often not told you the truth when you've asked how things were going because I didn't want you to know, I didn't want you to think less of me. I have desperately wanted to know what you know; I've never had the courage to ask.

"I know I'm whining. I don't expect you to wave a magic wand and everything will be okay. I just don't understand why my life has been so difficult when all around me I see others enjoying great success.

"Sometimes I feel like I just want to run away. The problem with that is I have to take me along wherever I go and all I want to do is to get away from me.

"I have allowed misplaced ego and false pride to prevent me from asking my best friend for guidance.

"No more. I have finally hit bottom. Now you know how bad it is, I'm asking for help.

"Does this make any sense at all to you?"

Chapter 4

I had been talking for more than two hours. Hugh had not interrupted once, nor did his gaze ever leave my face.

When I was finished he leaned forward, and stared past me to the side as if he was composing his response.

Finally he looked back at me and began "You know Earl, there is nothing in what you have just said that I didn't know.

"I have watched you battle your demons for more than thirty years and I've prayed for the day when you would come to me for help. I could have helped you years ago but I knew you weren't ready to listen.

"I have ached at watching your struggles but I knew that if I offered to help you would view that as just another failure of yours. So I have sat on the sidelines and watched my best friend tear himself to shreds year after year.

"I also knew that you would not come to me until you believed you had hit bottom, until you were in so much pain that you would do anything, including telling me what I've long known, in the hopes of making the pain go away.

"When you called me the other day I knew my prayers had finally been answered, that you would let me share with you those things that have brought so much joy into my life.

"You're the brother I never had. I couldn't love you more, or be closer to you than I would be if we were of the same blood, so thank you for coming to me, finally."

He knew all along? How could I have not known this?

"What I'm going to tell you will not be new to you. But what it means will rock your very being and, if you accept it, will allow you to completely reshape the rest of your life.

"Are you sure you're ready to let go of what you have because, as painful as it has been for you, it is exactly what you have wanted to this point in your life?

"I know that sounds ridiculous but it will make perfect sense in a little while so let me ask again, are you sure you're ready to let go of what you have?"

I stared at him in disbelief. Did he not hear a word I said? Did he not listen to story after story of failure and heartbreak? Did he not hear me describe how much pain I have lived with year after year? He couldn't have been listening or he wouldn't be telling me that the life I have is the life I want.

That's insane.

I guess he took my silence to mean yes because he continued.

"When we were born we arrived here laden with the most precious gifts imaginable. God gave us the gift of life, the gift of breath, the gifts of our senses, the gift of thought and so many more.

"But there is one gift that was bestowed upon us that far surpasses all of the other gifts combined. It is a gift so vast in potential, so massive in its flexibility, so complex in its structure that we often fail to understand how simple and far reaching it is in its application.

"How we use this gift determines the strength and quality of the foundation upon which our entire life is built.

"Most of us are aware of this gift at a cognitive level. We know about it, we know what it is but we don't grasp the totality of its role in every aspect of life.

"This gift determines our finances, our relationships, our careers, our education, our personal growth, our spiritual growth, our physical health, our emotions, everything.

"Every result in our lives has come from this gift and it is only by learning, understanding and applying this gift that we can have any chance of creating the lives we want.

"This gift is the very tool that we all use to sculpt our lives. It is never the tool itself that determines the quality of the sculpture; that is determined by how the tool is used.

"And what is this gift, this amazing gift that hides in plain sight from so many of us, that is the compass to our destination and the driving force behind our travels?

"It is our incredible gift of choice.

"And," he paused, looked straight at me and continued, "each of us has mastered its use."

He sat back, allowing me to let this sink in.

"You expected more, didn't you?" Hugh asked, sensing my disappointment. "But", he continued, "take a few minutes to think through what I just said, then ask yourself 'what else could there possibly be?' I think you will very quickly realize that that's all there is.

"And," he leaned forward with that Hugh grin on his face, "I'm going to spend the next few days teaching you just how big that little 'all' is."

Chapter 5

I wasn't sure what to think. I felt disappointed. It just seemed too simple.

"Are you telling me that if I had made different choices throughout my life, my life would have turned out very differently?"

"That's exactly what I'm telling you," he said. "The slightest difference in the choices we make will profoundly influence the largest differences in the end results.

"Let me give you an example. Imagine for a moment that you are out hiking on a trail. Suddenly the weather takes a nasty turn, the sky turns dark, the temperature drops alarmingly, a thick fog rolls in and you realize, with horror, that you do not have the clothing, food or equipment to survive a long, cold night out in the open.

"You turn on your cell phone and see that you have no service. Your decision to go on this hike was a spontaneous, last minute one and no-one knows you are out here. You feel yourself starting to panic.

"You flash back to that moment a few hours earlier, as you were leaving home, when that thought flashed through your mind about packing a few supplies and you had looked up at the perfectly blue, clear sky and chosen not to waste the few minutes it would have taken to collect what you now desperately need.

"A small choice, a massive consequence.

"Or consider the person who makes the choice that he is sober enough to drive when he shouldn't, and kills an innocent victim. A different choice would have saved a life.

"So you see Earl every single result in our lives begins to form itself the instant we make a choice. Sometimes that result is immediate and sometimes it might be weeks or even years distant.

"We need to consider not only our choices but their consequences.

"So let's see where else our choices affect our lives."

Chapter 6

"There really is only one thing that separates us as human beings, that makes you different from me and me different from everyone else. And it is that one thing that sets the direction for where life will lead us.

"And that one thing that accounts for all and every difference between us is this; it is what we as individuals believe to be true.

"It's as simple as that.

"Outside of the obvious differences between people, gender, age, ethnicity, physical attributes and capabilities that is all there is that makes us different.

"And yet those differences in our beliefs, sometimes just tiny, little differences, can have a profound affect on what happens in our lives.

"And every belief we have has become our belief because we exercised our gift of choice and chose to believe it.

"The first step in understanding why we are the way we are is to understand how we have formed our beliefs and then to recognize the influence our beliefs have over the decisions we make and the actions we take.

"In order to form a belief we first have to have something upon which to base a belief – we need to have information.

"That information can come to us through any number of different sources. It might come to us through a conversation with friends, a story in the media, a book we read or any other way in which we engage the world around us. It may come to us as a thought that pops into our head or even as a feeling.

"Let's examine a few possibilities.

"Perhaps we see a story on the news – a local politician is involved in a corruption scandal or a friend tells us of a bad experience she had in a restaurant or you are late for work because you couldn't find your car keys.

"Each of these represents both an experience in our lives as well as a source of information. Let's look at them individually and see what happens.

"A TV news report spoke of a scandal involving a local politician. Does this influence your belief about that politician, or perhaps all politicians? Does it confirm what you already thought about that politician?

"You see, all the story did was provide you with some information that there is an alleged scandal and that this politician may be involved.

"If, as a result of watching that story you now believe that politician is involved in this scandal and is corrupt, it tells us that you created that belief because you chose your interpretation of that news story to mean that politician is corrupt.

"In other words, the meaning you assigned to that story became your belief about that politician and because it is now your belief, it must also be true.

"But what if you had paused for a moment to consider other possible meanings of this story? Could a different meaning have left you with a different belief?

"Let's explore a few different meanings. Perhaps you know this politician personally, have worked on his campaigns, voted for him and believe strongly in his integrity.

"Another meaning may be that this politician has been set up by a political opponent, or the reporter is biased or there are two sides to a story or there could be many other meanings or interpretations you could place on this story and any different choice on your part would have resulted in a different belief.

"There is a wonderful old saying that says that there is no such thing as good news or bad news – just news. We choose whether it's good or bad.

"The same process applies to your friend who had a bad experience in a restaurant. Once you receive the information from her you will place your own meaning on it and that will become your belief.

"So you could choose her information to mean that you won't go to that restaurant or that one person's experience is not enough to influence your opinion or that she is never satisfied, finds fault with everything and that her story is probably more a reflection of her than a reasonable evaluation of that restaurant.

"Regardless of which meaning you select, the one you choose will become, or add to, your belief about that restaurant, or your friend, or both and will remain your belief until you choose to place a different meaning on that information.

"And the third example too is about an experience you had and how the meaning you choose for that experience will become, or reaffirm, your belief.

"You couldn't find your keys and spent twenty minutes searching everywhere before discovering them under an envelope on your coffee table.

"Now you're in your car, racing to work, and telling yourself over and over again what a disorganized idiot you really are.

"You remind yourself of other times when you have made mistakes and replay each of those in your head, constantly punctuating each scene with hurtful words to remind yourself how successful you are at being a failure.

"You already had the strong belief that you are incompetent and this episode of misplaced keys is simply a little more ammo to strengthen that belief.

"But are you incompetent? Are you consistently all of those painful, critical things you keep saying to yourself? Or have you just become so accustomed, so self-trained, to believe poorly of yourself that you seek every opportunity to pounce on any experience in your life that strengthens that belief?

"The real question then is where did that belief come from, where did it start?

"My guess is a long time ago, perhaps when you were a little child, you did something; perhaps you came home without your mitts, and your mother scolded you for this. And, perhaps during that reprimand she said something like 'you never pay attention' or 'if you don't smarten up you'll never amount to anything.'

"And you listened to what was being said and you decided that you will never be good at anything or that you will always mess up.

"What you did was to take that reprimand, and probably many others over the years and interpret them to mean just that - you will always fail. And so the meaning you gave that event became the belief you had about yourself at that time and, since then, you have worked diligently to strengthen that belief at every opportunity.

"What's important to recognize is that you, all by yourself, chose to place that meaning on what your mother said to you. Regardless of the words she said or the way in which she said the words, you interpreted that to mean what you now believe to be true about yourself.

"What might have happened if you had chosen a different meaning for what your mother said to you? Is it possible you would have created a whole different belief about yourself?

"If you had interpreted that event to mean that your mom really loved you and wanted only the best for you so this was her way of teaching you to be more responsible, is it possible you would have chosen a different belief?

"Or if you chose it to mean that your mother was just having a bad day and didn't mean any of the things she said about you, would that meaning have led to a different belief?

"The answer to both those questions is yes. Had you placed different meanings on all of those times you were reprimanded, you would have chosen different beliefs about yourself and your capabilities.

"As a child you couldn't possibly have understood the role you unwittingly played in building your beliefs about yourself. But, starting right now, you can take every single belief you have, hold it up to the light for examination, and if it is not helping you move in the direction you want your life to take, you can change the belief as rapidly as you chose to choose the meaning you placed on the events in your life that first created that belief.

"So Earl, the first step in creating a new life for yourself is to recognize the degree to which your beliefs have led to your present reality and that you can choose to change your beliefs with the same lightning speed you used when you chose them?

"Are you ready to believe that you can?"

Chapter 7

I opened my mouth to answer the question but Hugh held up his hand, gesturing for me to wait.

"Before you answer my question there is one more thing I need to add. You said earlier that you have finally hit bottom and that's why you are asking for help.

"I need you to understand a very important fact about yourself. And that fact is you haven't hit bottom. You're not even close. The funny thing is that so often, just when we start to think we have reached bottom, life will teach us that bottom is still a lot further down than we thought.

"You will only reach bottom the moment you start reaching for the top.

"And, Earl, in order to begin reaching for the top you must change some of those beliefs you have spent your lifetime developing, strengthening and validating, because if you don't you will continue to be surprised at how far down it is possible to go.

"Hugh," I stammered, "I really hadn't thought of it like that. Is it really as simple as you say to change the beliefs that I have had for so long?"

"Well, it is and it isn't. Sometimes just a new piece of information is enough to cause us to change a deeply entrenched belief and other times it may require some real hard work and commitment to do that.

"Let me give you an example of each.

"Let's revisit that politician who was alleged to be involved in a scandal and you chose not to believe a word of it because of your existing beliefs about that person.

"A few months later there is a story on the news showing that politician being led out of his office in handcuffs followed by a video clip taken with a hidden camera, showing him accepting a large sum of cash from an undercover police officer posing as a local developer and assuring him that all opposition to his proposed development would now, magically, disappear within a few days.

"Following the video clip is an interview with the person who had initiated the police investigation – a well known local developer - by complaining that this politician had told him that a project he was planning to build would never get off the ground unless he made substantial cash 'donation' to our favorite politician.

"It's quite likely, Earl, that the meaning you place on this new piece of information, this seemingly irrefutable, damning evidence is all that is needed to change your beliefs about him regardless of how strong that belief might have been.

"Does that make sense?"

"Absolutely," I replied, "but that type of belief seems quite different from the beliefs I have about me."

"It is very different," Hugh acknowledged, "and the differences lie in how you acquired the belief and how you continue to strengthen it.

"This will make perfect sense after we look at a different example.

"Let's assume for a moment that you have a belief about yourself that you will never amount to anything.

"And let's say that you have had that belief for as long as you can remember and that you have been telling yourself this for many years.

"Now let's pretend for a moment that every time, from a very early age, that each time, instead of telling yourself that you will never amount to anything, you had picked up a 10 pound dumbbell and done ten bicep curls with your left arm.

"How well developed would your left arm be now?"

"Extremely well developed," I answered, beginning to see where he was going with this.

"And your right arm," he enquired?

"Pitiful," I said sheepishly, "kind of like how it is now."

"Exactly," Hugh said with a grin, "and if you did ten curls with your right arm now, would that bring your right arm to the same state of development as your left?"

30

"No, of course not," I said, "I see exactly what you're saying. In the first example I can change my belief because it's relatively easy to examine the new information about the politician, which is awfully compelling, and I can easily attach a meaning that literally wipes out my previous belief about him.

"In the second example, the arm curls are a metaphor for my limiting belief and by 'working out' so diligently over the years, I have stacked these, one on top of the next so that this belief has become very strong and well developed.

"And the reason why you asked whether doing one set of curls with my right arm would cause it to be as strong and well developed as my left is because I have spent so many years developing my left arm that it is unrealistic to think that one set of curls on the other side could possibly lead to an equally well developed arm.

"See," I continued with a smug smile, "I'm not as stupid as I look."

"I wouldn't go that far," Hugh countered with a smile, "but you are on the right track. If your brain is like a muscle, you have exhibited tremendous discipline in continuing to train it to believe that you will never amount to anything.

"And not only have you trained your brain, you have taught yourself to accept as truth all those strong feelings of self loathing and helplessness that you experience each time you remind yourself that you'll never amount to anything.

"The sad truth for so many of us is that we work so hard, so diligently, with great discipline at training ourselves to excel at heartbreak."

I suddenly realized the room was getting darker. I glanced out the window. Day had turned into evening. We had been talking for more than eight hours without a break.

Chapter 8

"You know," Hugh said, shoveling baked French onion soup into his mouth, the melted cheese gyrating wildly between the spoon and his mouth, "it's fascinating how hard we will fight for our beliefs without realizing we are doing so."

It was a little after 8:00pm and we were having dinner at a quaint family owned bistro a few blocks from the hotel. We had realized the need to get away from each other for a while. Hugh had gone for a run while I had propped myself up on the couch in my room and allowed the days input to filter through my mind.

I realized Hugh was correct in everything he had said, and to prove him right, I spent an hour berating myself for having chosen the beliefs upon which I had built so much misery.

I continued to beat myself up until he returned.

"I'm starting to realize," I acknowledged, "how right you are in what you have been saying to me, and I now understand how much I have contributed to the development of my own limiting beliefs and how, in order to prove to myself that those beliefs are valid, I have consistently, throughout my life, made choices that have led to results in my life that have proven my beliefs to be true.

"As painful as it is to say this, I now understand that I am exactly where I want to be. I truly am a self made man.

"So, Sagacious One," I continued, making an attempt at levity that I certainly did not feel, "how do I turn back the clock and start over?"

"I haven't figured out the part about turning the clock back yet," Hugh replied with a smile, "but," he paused, his tone turning serious, "you can start over. That is a choice that you can make right now. Is that something you are willing to do?"

"I guess so," I relied lamely

"I guess so?" he said, mimicking the same flat monotone I had used, "I guess so? If that is your real answer then I don't think you are willing to start over and I'll tell you why.

"There are some conditions on making that choice that you need to know about. Do you remember I told you that the only possible way of knowing we have hit bottom is when we have had enough and start reaching for the top?

"Then listen carefully because there is nothing I can tell you that is more profound than what I am about to say. And just because you are listening to what I say does not mean that you are hearing what I say so, Earl, focus like you have never focused before. Focus as if the rest of your life depends on what happens in the next few minutes because," he looked straight at me as seriously as I have ever seen, "it does.

"Every manageable event, every controllable result in your life takes place in your head before it happens anywhere else. Not only does it take place in your head, it also takes place in your heart at the same time. The way you choose to frame it in your head and the feelings you choose to surround it with become the predictors, actually the guarantors of the end result.

"I know you're thinking that there must be more. It can't be that simple. You've always been a cynic and that part of you is resisting these words so let me explain.

"The reason why the results in our lives are pre-determined by the thoughts in our heads and the feelings in our hearts is really quite simple.

"Our lives are never static, they are dynamic. We are always in motion and if we are always moving then, it stands to reason, we must be heading somewhere.

"Therefore the direction we are heading towards is determined by what we do, by the actions we are taking. We have already agreed that the results in our lives come from what we do, or don't do, so we are always moving towards what we want or away from what we want.

"And what we do, those actions we take, is entirely governed by our feelings. Our feelings dictate what we do and, more importantly, how we do what we do.

"Yes, there are times when we do things we don't feel like doing, because we have to do them. But it's not just what we do that determines results; it's how we do it. I'm sure you'll agree that when we do those things we don't feel like doing, like visiting your mother-in-law when you'd rather be watching the game on TV, or dealing with a difficult client when you'd rather be meeting with an appreciative one. We don't do them with the same passion, the same commitment, the same motivation and the same desire for excellence as when we are doing the things we want to be doing.

"Reluctance breeds sub-standard performance every time. And remember, reluctance, like everything else, is a choice we have made.

"Earl, when I asked you if you are willing to start over and you said 'I guess so' there was no conviction behind those words. You weren't thinking it in your head and you certainly weren't feeling it in your heart.

"Your behaviour will always be congruent with what you think in your head and feel in your heart.

"Does any of this make sense to you?"

"It all makes sense to me Hugh. It just seems like such a huge task to begin recreating me at this stage of my life. It feels like I have to do a tremendous amount of work. I'm not sure that I have it in me to pay that kind of price. I don't know if I have the energy."

"I know how you feel," he acknowledged gently, "the task seems monumental. It seems so big that you can never get there. So perhaps I can help you change your perspective by looking at this from a different angle.

"You said that you don't know if you can pay the price, it seems so high. A long time ago I learned an old saying that has stuck with me through the years and has often helped me make the right choice when I have been faced with a difficult decision. It goes like this; 'in life there are always two prices to pay. There is the price of doing something and the price of doing nothing.

"You will pay one of them.

"Earl, for you the real question is which price will you pay? Are you willing to pay the price of starting over or will you continue to pay the price of seeking bottom? Are you willing to start moving towards where you want to be or will you continue moving closer to where you don't want to be?"

I was stunned by the question. I really hadn't thought of my life in those terms. I began to realize that I had been spending my entire life as a helpless victim, always questioning why the whole world seemed to be conspiring against me, why the only luck I ever had was bad luck when, in fact, my whole life had been playing out like a symphony and, all along, I had been the conductor.

"You're so right," I blurted out, "I am paying the price and it's bleeding me dry."

By now we had finished our meals and were sipping coffee. It had been a long day and I was feeling beaten up and emotionally exhausted.

Hugh, apparently, wasn't done with me yet.

"The first step," he began, "in reaching for the top is to begin the process of countering those well developed 'muscles' you have spent a lifetime building. You know the one's I mean?"

"Sure," I nodded, "how could I forget?"

"The world is full of experts and gurus who will tell you that changing those negative beliefs you have is an easy process. Well, I have spent a lifetime searching for the 'easy' method of overcoming years of crushing self criticism and I can assure you it is as mythical as a unicorn.

"If you are sincere about reaching for the top, if you want long term, sustainable change in your beliefs, if you want to replace self doubt with supreme confidence, defeat with victory, self hate with love and fear of failure with the certainty of success, you must begin training your brain and heart to feel all of these. You must build a new 'muscle' that is so much bigger and stronger than the one you have built that it will obliterate the old one each time it rears its ugly head.

"This is going to be hard work, but no harder than you have been working in developing the other one.

"So here's the plan. Tomorrow morning you're on your own. I have some personal stuff to attend to so we'll meet at noon and continue from there. Here's what you're going to do. As soon as you get back to your hotel room this evening, make a list of up to ten things that you would like to believe about yourself.

For example your list could include statements like 'I love myself. I am filled with confidence in my abilities. I am a gifted communicator. I enjoy magnificent health.'

"The key is to list only positive, powerful statements and to express them as if they are already part of you, as if you own them right now.

"What you're doing is compiling a list of affirmations. Are you familiar with those?"

"Sure", I answered, "I've often heard about the value of affirmations, I've have never used them. Do they work?"

"Well," he replied, "I've also heard about their value and, frankly, I think it's nonsense. If you tell yourself that you feel fantastic, and you say it in a passionless, dull monotone, I don't believe for one minute that it will invoke any strong, powerful feelings within you."

Hugh shrank down in his seat, his head moved down, his gaze shifted from my face to the floor, his expression flattened and in as dull and emotionless a voice tone as I have ever heard come out of his mouth he said, "I love myself. I love myself. I love myself."

I burst out laughing at the absurdity of his demonstration. It felt good to laugh.

"Affirmation without confirmation is defamation. When you tell yourself something about yourself without confirming the truth of it with your feelings you are lying to yourself about yourself.

Hugh continued, "It's not just what you affirm to yourself that makes a difference, it's how you affirm those things to yourself that have lasting affect.

"Just think of the emotions you have evoked each time you have told yourself how useless you really are and how real and present they were."

He was right, of course. I vividly remembered those feelings of hopelessness and despair I had felt those many, many times when I had plied myself with deafening, critical self talk. I realized how passionate and convincing I had been in my condemnation of myself and how effective the results had been.

"I hadn't realized how good I am at self destruction," I said as the far reaching consequences of my 'skill' began to sink in, "I guess I really have world class sales skills, I've sure sold me on my inadequacies."

"You certainly are talented," Hugh agreed, "now you need to put that talent to work to design and sculpt the life you really want.

"I want you to spend tomorrow morning working on you. I mentioned I have some stuff to do. We'll continue when I'm done, some time after noon. Your job is to spend the morning feeling everything you put onto that list we just talked about.

"And what I mean by feeling that list is that it's really important to bring every word on that list to life. So, walk around your room, say each line over and over until you absolutely feel the truth of each statement throughout your body. Act as if every word of every sentence is real. Smile, stand tall and speak with a tone of conviction. And each time you start to doubt what you're doing, each time you feel silly talking to yourself remember to remind yourself of three things.

"Number one, you've been doing this for years, you're just changing the message, number two, there are always two prices to pay so choose wisely and number three you're always moving towards where you want to be. You choose which direction that is by what you put in your head and what you feel in your heart.

"Choose wisely, my friend."

Chapter 9

I awoke the next morning with a feeling of excited anticipation that I hadn't felt in so long I had trouble recognizing it.

I was energized, focused and radiating positive intention as I hurriedly showered, dressed, called room service, ordered a gallon of coffee and prepared to begin my new life.

The only time I could remember ever feeling this invigorated had been fifteen years earlier. I had undergone surgery to remove a growth from my left lung.

For four years prior to the surgery my health had deteriorated to the point where crossing a street required planning and frequently left me exhausted and gasping for breath on the other side. I had been unable to work and had experienced homelessness and street life for a short while.

Ironically one phone call to Hugh would have solved that problem but pride, or should I say false pride, had prevented me from making the call.

The day before surgery I had been given a device called an incentive spirometer which has a mouthpiece to blow into and three little balls that are on the bottom. The objective is to blow into the mouthpiece and raise the balls as high as possible. I was unable to raise the balls off the bottom of the device. I had been told there was a high possibility I would not survive the surgery.

I vaguely remember waking up in the ICU afterwards and talking to one of the nurses. What I do remember with crystal clarity is her giving me my spirometer and seeing the balls rise to the top and stay there for some ten seconds or longer and the incredible feeling of joy that coursed through my whole body.

I had been given a new lease on life and what a feeling that was.

And that's exactly the feeling I felt that morning in my hotel room.

A second new lease on life.

I had come back to my room after dinner and spent an hour or so writing my list. I had ploughed through the feelings of foolishness and had ignored that irritating voice in my head that kept telling me I was wasting my time.

Remembering Hugh's instruction I had written and rewritten the list until I could actually read each sentence and begin to feel its meaning. I had fallen asleep on the couch while reading it for the billionth time and had woken at around 3:00am long enough to crawl into bed and sleep for a few more hours.

While waiting for my coffee to arrive I picked up my list and read it again. Hugh had suggested my list have up to ten statements, I had settled for four that just felt right. I thought this was an excellent start.

I chuckled to myself as I thought of what would have been on my old list:

> You're a loser
>
> You'll never amount to anything
>
> Why bother, you'll just fail anyway
>
> It'll never work

I forced my thoughts back to my new list and stopped myself from thinking of the old one as Hugh's voice came into my head and sternly reminded me that the direction I move towards is always determined by my thoughts.

"Yikes," I remember saying out loud, "old habits die hard."

My coffee arrived; I gulped down a cup, poured a second and went to work.

I can't say that I felt much conviction as I paced the room, forcing a smile onto my face, thrusting my shoulders back and reading my affirmations over and over. In fact, I felt dishonest. I felt I was lying to myself.

Suddenly a thought popped into my head. How would I feel if everything on my list was true? I stopped pacing and felt myself being absorbed into that question. As I focused on the answer a funny thing happened. The cloak of silliness began to drift away and was replaced by strong feelings of confidence, strength and love.

I was filled with excitement as the realization of what had just happened began to sink in. These incredible feelings of empowerment had permeated my very being just by thinking about them.

For the first time in such a long time I felt that I was in charge, that I had absolute control over my feelings. I had that feeling – you know the one, when you just know that you know – that my life had changed forever and that from now on I would be making far better choices which would lead to far better results in my life.

I resumed pacing but this time I felt the truth of every affirmation on my list. My voice resonated with conviction as I recited each sentence over and with such determination that it was as if I was determined to fully develop that 'muscle' in just one morning.

I couldn't wait for Hugh to show up with the next lesson.

Chapter 10

"Well, are you a changed man?" Hugh asked with a grin as I opened the door to let him in.

"Because if you are then this is for you." He handed me the tray he had been carrying. "I picked it up on my way through the lobby. I figured if you had been doing your homework you should be ready for something to eat and if you haven't well, you may as well eat it anyway because we'll have nothing to talk about."

"I am kind of hungry," I said, "I have been working on myself for almost four hours and I think I've walked the equivalent of a marathon just in this room. I have even come up with a name for this. I call it my affirmathon. You know, like a telethon where people call in their pledges? My affirmathon is when I pledge powerful affirmations to myself."

I handed the food tray back to him. "To tell you the truth I'm too excited to be hungry. What's next?"

"Affirmathon? I like that. Now tell me everything that's happened," he said, placing the tray on the bed, "I'm really interested to know what has changed from yesterday."

"Ok," I began," handing him my list, "I spent some time last night working on this until I felt that I had really captured the essence of who and what I want to be. I chose these four statements because as I wrote them they just felt right."

I filled him in on every detail taking care to point out with pride how in just a few hours I had developed the ability to influence my own feelings simply by what I thought and by what I told myself.

I talked about focusing through the feelings of doubt I had experienced when I first began repeating my affirmations and how quickly I had learned that by adjusting my body position, facial expression and voice tone I could change my feelings and therefore my perception in seconds.

Hugh listened without interruption. I could tell by his expression that he was proud of the progress I'd made and that gave me an immense feeling of accomplishment.

As I was enjoying the feeling I realized Hugh was teaching me yet another lesson; take every victory, every success, no matter how small and bask in it. Stack each success on top of the previous one, real or imagined. Each little piece makes the pile bigger, stronger and more real.

When I was finished Hugh looked up at me with the biggest smile I have ever seen. "Wow, I cannot believe the change in you since yesterday. If you had said everything you just told me in a foreign language I would be just as aware of how different you are. I haven't heard that much life in your voice in years and I can't remember the last time I saw such animation in your expression. I am absolutely thrilled for you.

"You have gained remarkable momentum now promise me that you will commit to affirming your greatness to yourself a minimum of four times each day for at least ten minutes each time.

"I promise," I stated without hesitation. Why wouldn't I. It feels so good.

"That's great," he concluded and added with a grin, "three months from now you are going to be magnificently insufferable."

I ate my lunch as Hugh told me of how his morning had been spent scouring local stores searching for the perfect graduation gift for Lauren, his granddaughter. He pulled a beautiful, intricate bracelet out of his pocket and proudly showed me the inscription he'd had engraved on the back.

'Usquequaque illic, Gramps.'

"We have covered a lot of ground since yesterday and we still have a lot of work to do. Let's take a few minutes and recap what we have accomplished so far.

"We talked about the all powerful gift that God gave us at birth, the wonderful gift of choice and the far reaching implications that gift has in determining the results we will experience in our lives.

"We use that gift to choose everything that we believe to be true and those beliefs govern the direction in which we point our lives and play a significant role in our choice of actions which have led us to where we are today.

"We agreed that our beliefs are like muscles – the more we work at developing them, the bigger and stronger they become.

"And then we agreed that the first step to changing what happens in your life is to change your beliefs about what will happen. We talked about the price of doing nothing and changing nothing versus the price of changing beliefs and thereby changing results and we agreed that either way we are paying a price, so we may as well pay the price of change and begin moving in the direction of where we want to be.

"You agreed to start developing new belief "muscles" and have, in a very short time, made enormous progress in that direction.

"Does that about sum it up?" "Are you ready to move on?"

Chapter 11

"Yes, I am," I answered, anxious for the next lesson.

"Alright," said Hugh, "then let's get started. I'm a huge believer in setting goals. I believe planning is to success what breath is to life. You can't have one without the other.

"All my life I have set goals for myself and developed a plan to lead me to them.

"I am convinced this is crucial for a number of reasons.

"A plan establishes a target to aim for, a direction in which to point yourself. A plan sets you on course and helps keep you there. And it lets you know if you drift off course.

"I have developed a planning model that I call On Course that I have used for many years in my own life and have been sharing with my clients for the last few years. So let's put it to work for you.

"The first step in planning is to know what you want, to establish your goal. This is important because your goal becomes your destination; it determines the direction in which you will be heading.

"Remember, we have many different areas in our lives and the process of goal setting is the same for each of them. So Earl, take a few minutes and think of one goal you would like to accomplish in any area of your life."

My mind immediately flashed to my financial and business challenges but after a moment's reflection my mind was invaded by competing desires from almost every area of my life and Hugh, obviously sensing my dilemma gently intervened. "Just pick one, and we'll work through the process. You'll have plenty of time to get to the others later."

I felt myself relaxing as my focus drifted through the list of my goals, finally settling on one that had been a lifelong source of frustration for me. I told Hugh and he nodded knowingly.

"That's really what you want?" he asked. "Then let's talk about it.

"If this truly is your goal, if it's what you really want then we move on to the next question which is what is your prize?"

"What do you mean," I asked, puzzled?

"Most people assume that their goal is what they really want. My experience has taught me otherwise. The real question is this 'what will achieving your goal mean to you?'

"You see Earl, when we say we want something it's because we believe that getting that 'something' will provide us with something else. I know that sounds confusing so let me give you an example.

"Let's say your goal is a something material. You want a brand new Mercedes. So, what will getting a new Mercedes do for you?

"Perhaps it will make you feel successful. Perhaps you think others will be impressed when they see you driving it. Perhaps you will feel safe because of its many safety features.

"Rarely will a person tell you they want a new Mercedes as a means of transportation, the prize is invariably a feeling, a feeling of being successful or impressing others of feeling safe. So it is really important to know what your prize is, rather than just simply identifying your goal. Does that make sense?"

"I think so," I answered, "in the example of a material goal that makes sense; can you give me another example?

"Sure. Your goal is to succeed your boss as vice president when he retires next year. What will becoming a vice president mean to you?

"Perhaps it means that you will now have greater influence in the direction the company takes. Perhaps you just want a bigger office. Perhaps you believe this will earn you respect in the eyes of other. There are a million possible 'perhaps' and you believe that each one of them will give you a feeling that you want.

"I get it," I said. "This ties in with everything you've been telling me. Our beliefs, those things that we accept as being 'facts' have profound influence over our feelings, kind of like a cause and effect relationship so what you're saying is our goal is really a belief, and when we reach our goal, the real prize is how we feel. Am I correct?"

"You're an 'A' student," Hugh replied, "now you understand why it is so important to know what the prize is, because it's the prize that we really want. The goal is simply the switch that turns on our feelings.

"And sometimes when we do achieve our goal we discover that our belief was wrong."

"What do you mean," I asked, curious.

"There's an old expression that cautions us to be careful of what we ask for. Sometimes when we achieve our goals we feel a sense of disappointment. Our expectations of how we will feel are not met. Sometimes a Mercedes is just a means of transport, we don't feel successful driving it and no-one seems to notice anyway. And sometimes a bigger office is just more space in which to feel unfulfilled."

"As you can see, there's far more to setting goals than simply deciding what you want. It is absolutely necessary to ensure that getting what you want will give you what you want.

"Which is why the next question is the one most important of all and we should get right to it.

"So let's take a break."

Chapter 12

Hugh went to his room to return a few calls and I spent ten minutes pacing the room and doing my affirmathon before I collapsed on the couch to reflect on our conversation.

What a fascinating discussion. Hugh had helped to completely change my perspective on goal setting and the more I thought about it, the more sense it made.

I thought back to previous goals I had set and to how seldom I had reached them. I realized that a large part of my life had been spent in conflict as the goals I had set and the feelings I hoped to feel by achieving them were at war with my limiting beliefs that convinced me I would never amount to anything.

Some of us humans really excel at creating complexity from simplicity.

I knew in that moment that doing my affirmathon every day, several times each day, was the foundation upon which I could set and pursue my goals. Any other choice would be a poor one.

I closed my eyes and started thinking about my prize.

I had just finished writing it down when Hugh banged loudly on the door.

His first words as I opened the door were "Well, now that we've got the easy part behind us, let's tackle the hard part."

He sat down, poured a cup of coffee and began, "Here's what you've done to this point as far a goal setting goes; you have identified a goal you intend to achieve for yourself and, while I was gone you determined what the prize is, what reaching your goal will do for you."

I nodded in agreement.

"Now we come to what I believe is the most important question of all. Your answer to this next question will determine, more than anything else, the probability that you will stay with the plan, that you will do those things that we will identify shortly that are key to reaching your goal.

"It's a small word with gigantic consequences. And that word is 'why?' The question becomes 'why do you want that goal? Why is attaining the prize important to you?'

"I have gone through this process with many people and those experiences have taught me, without exception, that if you can't clearly articulate your reasons why you want this prize or these prizes, you will not stay the course. You will not reach your goal. You will give up.

"You see Earl, we only ever do one thing. We only do what's important to us in the moment and it's the accumulation of those 'one things' we do in the moment that will either steer us towards our goal or away from it."

I was confused. "I don't understand what you mean," I began. Hugh, obviously anticipating my response, continued.

"Let's try a few examples.

"Let's assume your goal is to lose weight. You have carefully selected a process for achieving that goal and are diligently following your plan.

"You're out for dinner with a group of friends. You have stayed faithful to your plan ordering a meal that meets all the requirements of you weight-loss regimen.

"After clearing away the dinner plates the server approaches your table and says these deadly words. 'Our dessert special this evening is beyond amazing. It is a double chocolate cheese cake smothered in raspberry sauce served with strawberry ice-cream. It is unbelievable. We only have four pieces left so I told the chef to hold them for you. Can I bring them out for you now or would you like to wait a few minutes?'

"With much excitement your friends all place their orders and the server looks at you. You love cheesecake, it's your favorite. You really love chocolate. In fact there is no word in our language to describe the love you have for cheesecake and chocolate together. You begin salivating. You really want that dessert.

"What are you going to do?

"Or perhaps you have joined a health club and committed to going there and working out three times a week. So far you have religiously kept this commitment but now, as you begin the second week of your commitment, all you want to do is go home and pass out on the couch. It's been a long, tough day. You didn't sleep well last night, you had to put in an extra couple of hours at the office to deal with an unexpected emergency, your back hurts, you have a headache and just getting to the couch will probably exhaust the little remaining energy you have left.

"But tonight is a scheduled gym night. What will you do?

"Or maybe you will relate to this example? You're a salesperson. You're in your office. You look at your calendar and realize that you do not have any scheduled sales appointments for the next three weeks.

"You know you should pick up the phone and start making sales calls but you just don't feel like doing that. Sales calls suck. You can't reach anyone because people use Caller I.D. and voicemail to screen their calls. When you do manage to get through, invariably some people will be extremely rude, some will just hang up on you and only a tiny percentage will agree to meet you. The constant rejection has worn you down but you understand that without appointments you can't sell anything and month end is coming soon and bringing all those bills along with it.

"You hate making those calls but you know you have to make those calls to survive and then, thankfully, you remember that proposal you need to prepare for a prospective client.

"Your meeting to present that proposal is two months away but you really enjoy preparing proposals. There's no stress.

"If you don't make calls, you won't sell anything and those month end bills still have to be paid. Phone calls are painful, proposals are fun.

"Which choice will you make?"

I stared at Hugh, not saying anything. I have lived each of those exact examples many, many times and I reflected on how I had rationalized my way to eating the cake, hitting the couch and writing brilliant proposals time and time again.

I had used the same pattern of thinking each time. I remember thinking that I'd have the cake now and absolutely go back to the program tomorrow. I'd lie on the couch and rest up today and go all out at the gym tomorrow. I'd get the proposal done today and hit the phones first thing tomorrow morning.

Yikes. The power of self delusion.

As if reading my thoughts, Hugh continued. "Sounds familiar doesn't it. Most of us can relate to those types of examples.

"The choice we make will always move us either closer to our goal or further away from it.

"The question is 'why?' Why do we make the choice we make when we know those aren't the actions we committed to?

"I told you a while ago that this question, the 'why' question is the most important of all.

"Not only do our reasons for wanting to achieve our goal and claim our prize have to be well articulated, they must be huge and compelling.

"Our reasons for doing what we need to do to achieve our goals have to be much bigger than our reasons for not doing those things. They have to be so big that they overwhelm all those other reasons.

"If we can't define our reasons, if we can't feel those reasons with such intensity and urgency that they become impenetrable, we will spend our lives building disappointment and frustration into our dreams.

"Earl, there really is only one reason why you gave up on your goals all those times in the past. It's because your reasons for not doing those things you knew should be done were bigger than your reasons for doing them. Period."

As much as it hurt to hear Hugh say that, as much as I wanted to open my mouth and tell him he was wrong, that this may be true for everyone else but my situation is different, that he doesn't understand, that he was oversimplifying, being cruel, didn't know what he was talking about, in my heart of hearts I knew he was correct.

"It hurts to hear this doesn't it," he asked? I nodded in agreement.

"Let me explain why," he continued.

"We only ever do one thing. We always do what is most important to us in the moment."

He paused, allowing that to sink in.

He said it again. "We only ever do one thing. We always do what is most important to us in the moment.

"You may well argue with what I've just said. Most people do. You can tell me that reaching your goals is extremely important to you and that you will do whatever it takes to get there. The truth is that, all too often with many people, their goals are only important until something more important in the moment, like the cheesecake, comes along and then it, the cheesecake, assumes a higher importance and because we only do what is important in the moment, we devour the cheesecake.

"Am I making any sense at all?

Chapter 13

"I'm not sure I'm ready to say it's not important to do what I have to do to reach my goals," I began but Hugh cut me off.

"I didn't say it's not important, I said it's not as important in the moment. What that means is that, at the moment when you chose to eat the cake, dive onto the couch or bury yourself in a proposal, you made that choice because it felt more important than the other choice available to you at that moment.

"Please understand that it is our feelings that will lead to our choices and those choices are determined by two very powerful but opposing forces.

"When we make a choice, cheesecake or not, gym or couch, phone calls or proposal, we will make our choice for one of two reasons. We choose what to do in order to either gain pleasure or to avoid pain.

"And as simplistic as it sounds, those two emotions govern every decision you have ever made and will ever make. All that varies from decision to decision, choice to choice is the intensity of the pain or pleasure.

"Take a moment, Earl and think about how you made your selection from the menu when we were having dinner last night."

I did just that. My mind flashed back to the restaurant and as I relived the moments I had spent studying the menu I realized that Hugh was absolutely correct.

Again.

I have long been a connoisseur of French onion soup and that was the first thing I had noticed when I opened the menu. I had mentally decided not to order the soup because I am trying to lose a couple of pounds, well actually, seventy, and I knew I'd be mad at myself afterwards.

I had also eyed a pasta dish described as 'swimming in a magnificent cream and brandy sauce' and had ruled that out in favor of a dinner sized salad garnished with grilled vegetables.

I had felt quite proud of my choice until the owner had come to our table to take our order. Hugh had asked him about the French onion soup and, with obvious pride, he had described every step of the preparation and how its reputation brought customers to his restaurant from all over the world.

As I listened I realized that I couldn't pass up this once in a lifetime opportunity to savor magnificence. We both ordered the soup and I felt hungry at the anticipation of its arrival.

I had ordered the French onion soup in order to experience the pleasure of culinary perfection (I hadn't been disappointed) and had ordered the salad in order to avoid pain as I accepted that the pasta dinner was not part of my eating regimen.

I sheepishly acknowledged this to Hugh and he explained further. "What happened last night was a graphic example of how we use our wonderful gift of choice. When you decided to order the soup, in that moment having that soup was more important to you than sticking to your program. I'm not saying that your program is not important to you, it's just that in that moment, as important as your weight loss program is to you, it became less important when pitted against the choice of world class French onion soup.

"In that moment your reasons for ordering the soup were bigger, stronger and more compelling than your reasons for not ordering it. Your feeling of gaining immediate pleasure outvoted your feelings of avoiding future pain.

"And we will always decide in favor of the stronger of those two feelings.

"Does it make sense now why it is so important to know clearly, unequivocally and unconditionally what your 'why' is if you are to have any chance of winning your prize?

"It sure does." I answered with a whole new sense of insight into my own life, "I had never thought of it like that. Why are we so weak that we can be so easily swayed?"

"It's not about being weak," Hugh responded, "it's about recognizing the role that gratification plays in our lives.

"We live in a culture where we want instant gratification. Just watch TV commercials. They all show us that if we buy the product we will immediately enjoy the benefit. Think of all those health and fitness infomercials. They 'guarantee' that if we use the product for just ten minutes, three times a week we will see results in 'just' ten days, or three weeks or thirty days. Imagine how inspired you would be if the infomercial told you that if you use the product three times a week for four hours each time you will have the body you want in three to five years. My guess is their sales would be zero or darn close.

"One of the fundamental truths of life is that sometimes, to enjoy the wonder of the view from the top of the mountain, you must endure the pain of forging a pathway through bushes and thorns on the way up.

"When we can gain instant pleasure we invariably will make that choice. Typically when we set goals, the attainment of those goals is quite far into the future. To experience the pleasure that achieving those goals will give us, we often have to endure pain like saying no to the cheesecake or the French onion soup, going and working out at the gym when we would rather zone out on the couch and 'suck up' the frustration of those phone calls when it is so much easier to work on a proposal, even when we know that by making those choices we are assuring ourselves of future pain, possibly even greater pain.

"In each of those examples we were faced with a choice that caused us pain. The pain of saying no to something we wanted - the cheesecake - or the pain of doing something we didn't 'feel' like doing - working out and making phone calls. So how did we make the pain go away? We chose to do something that gave us pleasure or caused less pain, despite knowing that our decision would cause us greater pain in the future.

"If you think of the third example, we chose to write a proposal because we didn't want to face the pain of making phone calls despite knowing that this decision would lead to even greater pain at the end of the month when we would not be able to pay our bills. This doesn't make any sense until we view this decision through the lens of immediacy. The pain of making calls is immediate, right now.

The pain of not being able to pay our bills is several days away. We live in the present moment so we take steps to make the immediate pain disappear.

"Many, if not most of us, will work harder and take more immediate action to make pain go away than we will to gain future pleasure.

"I have read many studies of successful people, people who have achieved great success by whatever means you choose to measure success and in each case there is an undeniable, irrefutable common thread. People who achieve great success have a unique ability to "suck it up", to endure pain, to do what they don't always feel like doing in the knowledge that ultimately the pain is simply part of the price of getting to their goals.

"They have mastered the ability to delay gratification until they succeed. In other words they are willing to pay the price that must be paid to get to where they want to be.

"They intuitively understand that they, by their choices and actions, are either moving towards their goals or away from them and so they choose to move towards the goals regardless of how much pain they have to endure in the short term."

"A long time ago I learned that there is no escape from the pain. We just create temporary diversions that push the pain away in the short term. I learned that there are two types of pain and we will experience one or the other.

"The first is called the pain of discipline. This is the pain we must become willing to endure if we want to reach our goals so badly that we will pay any price to get there. Discipline is the pain of endurance and it is always short term. The other pain is called the pain of regret and not only will it last much longer than the pain of discipline, but after we experience regret enough times our beliefs change and we choose to believe that it is not possible to achieve those goals so what's the point in even trying.

"At this point we give up. We have taught ourselves, through repeated disappointment, that it's hopeless. We have turned ourselves into victims of something called learned helplessness.

"All because we chose not to do what we knew we needed to do. The pain of regret is intense."

Hugh stood up. "I hope this is helpful. I have tried to live my life by these principles and they have stood me in good stead. Now it's your turn to shine. I think we should split up for the evening. You need to really explore and discover your compelling reasons for getting to the goal we discussed earlier. You do your homework and let's meet back here tomorrow morning."

I thanked him again for all his help and he left. I had learned another priceless lesson over the past few days. We don't need a lot of friends. If we have just one wonderful friend we are truly blessed.

I did something I haven't done in many years. I prayed. I sank to my knees and apologized to God for all those years of poor choices when I had been blessed with the choice of making better choices. I thanked Him for sending Hugh to help me and I promised to appreciate, and exercise wisely, my magnificent power of choice for the rest of my life.

I was filled with a cathartic sense that felt as if an enormous weight had miraculously been lifted off my shoulders and, for the first time in memory, I felt a calm peacefulness that I can only describe as serene.

I wanted to stay on my knees and enjoy that feeling forever.

I stayed in that position for several hours. I had a strong feeling that my life had changed in a way that I could only have hoped for previously.

When I finally got up on my feet the sun had gone down and my hotel room was dark. I had lost all track of time.

My task for the evening was to discover my true reasons for pursuing my goal but before I could begin that journey I had something equally important that needed to be done.

I sat on the couch and thought about my affirmathon. I stood and began my ritualistic pacing of the room repeating each line with such fervor that within a few moments I could feel the presence of each statement with an intensity that only true conviction can bring.

After a while I turned my attention to my key task for the evening. I asked myself why I wanted that goal, why I wanted what realizing that goal would do for me?

I had thought this would be easy. It wasn't. After some time I glanced at the list of reasons I had written on my note pad. Pretty lame. There was nothing on my list that was particularly inspiring.

Then I remembered something that Hugh had said earlier. He had said to pick a point in the future, five, ten, fifteen, even twenty years from now and project yourself to that time.

I chose ten years hence and began to focus on what my life would be like in ten years if I hadn't achieved my goal.

I thought not just of what it would be like ten years from now but also what the ten years would be like. I began to feel all the feelings of hopelessness, fear, frustration, pain, absence of happiness, just barely surviving. It really hurt.

And as I allowed myself to steep in my own misery I suddenly realized I had my reasons.

My reasons were the opposite feelings to those I was feeling at that moment.

Finally the light had gone on in my head. In his own subtle way Hugh had known our best learning's are the ones we teach ourselves. He had led me to the water. I had to choose to drink it.

I got it. To know what we want, we first have to be clear on what we don't want.

And our reason? Our why? No matter what tangible reason we tell ourselves, our real reason for wanting to win our prize always comes down to one thing. A feeling. To be happy.

It's so simple.

Achieving the goal = winning the prize.

Winning the prize = being happy.

And a lifetime of happiness is a choice.

There and then I chose to commit to happiness.

Chapter 14

I don't think I have ever had a more restful sleep.

By the time Hugh knocked on the door I had been up for several hours, dressed, 'affirmathoned' for fifteen minutes and had been out for a brisk thirty minute walk.

I felt good and I was ready for more.

Skipping all niceties Hugh got straight to the point. "So tell me your urgent, compelling reasons."

Hugh listened attentively as I explained my reasons, my 'whys.' When I was finished he sat quietly for a moment as if pondering what I had just said. Finally he looked up and asked, "are those reasons strong enough to keep you moving towards your goal regardless of how strong the pull to go the other way becomes?"

"I believe so," I replied, "each time I think of my reasons why I want to reach my goal, I feel a powerful strength within me that I know will guide me through those times when I don't feel like doing what I need to do."

"That's terrific," Hugh said, his head nodding in approval, "we have talked a lot about how achieving goals for most of us is less about learning what we have to do and more about doing what we know we must do in order to get there.

"There is a wonderful quote attributed to Aristotle that says, 'We are what we repeatedly do. Excellence, then, is not an act but a habit.'

"I believe what he was telling us is that we become the product of our habits. In order to win the prize we must develop the habits of doing those things that must be done to get us there.

"If we haven't been achieving our goals it's because we have developed the wrong habits. We have developed the habits of eating cheesecake and French onion soup, lying on the couch and writing proposals. We have developed the habit of giving in to pain.

"Our next step is to identify specifically what it is going to take for you to reach your goal. We need to be very clear on what you absolutely must do repeatedly to get there.

"When I ask people to make a list, or tell me everything they need to do to achieve a goal I am often astounded at how big the list is. Most people will include activities in their list that are either peripherally related to winning their prize or not connected to the prize at all.

"Let's say, for example, that your goal is to reach a measurable fitness level and, in order to get there, you have determined that you need to complete a particular training regimen at your health club three times each week.

"Getting to the gym requires planning and preparation on your part. You must arrange a baby-sitter for your kids, you need to plan your work schedule so that you can leave the office and get to the gym in time to do your program and you have to have use of the family car to get there.

"So your action list of what you believe is necessary to reach your goal contains four activities. Completing your program, arranging a baby-sitter, planning your schedule and making sure you have transportation to get you there.

"Each of those activities plays a role in you achieving your goal. Each is important in that any of them can prevent you from getting to the health club. But only one will move you closer to your goal.

"I call that one a directional activity.

"Directional activities are those things that directly move us towards our goals. There is a simple way of determining whether something is directional or whether it is merely important. Each time you complete a directional activity you are incrementally closer to your goal.

"You may only be a hair's width closer, but you are closer.

"I know that sounds confusing so let's look at your list. Arranging a baby sitter is very important. Without someone to watch the kids you may not be able to go to the gym. Planning your schedule is important so you can leave work in time to get to the gym. Having the car available is important to get you to the gym.

"A glitch in arranging any of these may well prevent you from getting to the gym but will any of them move you closer to your goal?

"The answer is 'no.' None of those activities will move you one millimeter closer to your goal. There is only one activity on your list that is directional and that is completing your workout regimen.

"The others are important but you can have all of them in place, get to the gym in good time and decide that you are too tired to workout and spend your time reading a magazine in the locker room.

"Earl, I have never gone through this process with anyone where the number of directional activities required to reach their goals has been more than six. In fact, I would guess that the average goal requires three or fewer directional activities.

"So do this; make a list of those things you need to do to reach your goal. Ask yourself this question, 'will I be closer to my goal each time I do this?' If the answer is yes you have a directional activity.

"I'm going to leave you for a while to think this through."

Interesting.

As I thought of all the different things I needed to do to get to my goal I put each one through the direction test. Will doing this move me closer to my prize? Once again Hugh was right. My new To Do list for achieving my goal had only three items.

I paced my room doing my affirmathon while waiting for Hugh to return. This was rapidly becoming my new favorite thing to do.

"Excellent job," Hugh affirmed after returning to the room and examining my new list. "Are you saying that doing these three activities repeatedly will lead you to your goal?"

"Sure will," I said with full confidence. "If I just do those three things I will definitely win my prize."

I noticed the look on Hugh's face and hastily added, "Won't I?"

"There's a little more to be done but you're definitely on the right track. In order to fully understand what is required of you to get to your goal there are a few more pieces to be added. You need to look at each activity and determine three things; frequency, intensity and duration.

"In other words look at the first activity on your list and ask yourself, 'how often do I need to do this in order to reach my goal, how much or how many must I do and for how long do I need to do this?

"Frequency will always apply to each activity; the other two will vary based on the activities you chose."

That made sense to me. I re-examined my list and played with those questions until I was satisfied.

By the time I was done, it was crystal clear. It was a blueprint for goal achievement.

And it was mathematical.

Activity X frequency + intensity + duration = prize.

It couldn't get simpler than that.

I showed Hugh my completed directional activities program. He slowly read through it then asked, "you're saying that this is what it will take for you to get to your goal. If you do exactly as you have described here, you will reach your prize, is that correct?"

"Yes it is." I answered.

"This is your game plan? Anything less and you won't get there or it will take longer, anything more is not necessary? Right?

"Yes" I said again.

"So if you just meet this plan you will succeed?

"Yes," I snapped, not even trying to hide the irritation I was beginning to feel.

How many more times was he going to ask the same question?

"So if you now know exactly what you have to do to win your prize, the real question, the million dollar question is, 'will you do it?

"Will you commit to yourself right now, now that you know what has to be done, that you will deliver on these activities exactly as you have written them until you reach your goal?'

"A long time ago," he continued, "I heard an expression that has stayed with me because it makes the point I'm trying to get to in a far better way than I can. The expression is 'everyone wants to go to heaven, but no-one wants to die.'

"That's the price of admission, there's no other way of getting there. So I guess what I'm asking you is this, 'are you willing to pay the price of getting to your goal?

"They say that there are always two prices we can pay, the price of doing something and the price of doing nothing."

He was so right. All our work over the past few days came down to this. And like everything else Hugh has told me, it will all come down to the choices I make.

Saying yes was more than telling Hugh I would do this. I realized that by saying yes I was making an unbreakable promise to myself.

And it was a big one.

I was promising me that I would create new habits, that I would endure the pain of doing what I didn't feel like doing when and if that happened. I would master the pain of discipline and avoid the pain of regret. These new rituals would carve out a beautiful new life for me.

And I would do this while meeting all the other daily demands life places on us.

There really was only one possible choice.

I smiled at Hugh, "you have taught me that the results in our lives come from the choices we make." I stood and placed my right hand over my heart, "I hereby pledge to choose the pathway to happiness."

We both laughed.

Chapter 15

Hugh was scheduled to fly home that evening. He took off to meet up with a few old friends and I was left alone with my thoughts.

So much had happened in such a short time. As I reflected over the past few days I was amazed at the changes in me. If someone had told me that I would shift from defeated to excited, from hopelessness to certainty and from directionless to laser focus, I would not have believed them for a second.

I began to plan for tomorrow – the first day of my new life. I had major decisions to make including deciding what to do with my existing business and how to dig myself out of the debt hole I had crawled into.

I knew it was not going to be easy. There was a lot of pain in my future, a lot to endure between where I was today and where I wanted to be. I felt ready for it.

It was a wonderful feeling of empowerment to look to the future without feelings of fear and trepidation. I felt invigorated by the challenges of designing my new life and then constructing it to my exact specifications.

I reached under the bed and retrieved the bag I had placed there. I carried it into the bathroom and gleefully disposed of its contents with several strategic flushes of the toilet.

I could not believe that I had ever had those thoughts.

As I settled on the couch to wait for Hugh to get back I was struck by a fascinating realization.

When I had checked into the hotel a few days ago my life was a shambles. My business was failing, again, my marriage was teetering, my health was marginal and my state of mind was bleak. I had felt defeated, suicidal, alone, exhausted and helpless.

Now, a mere three days later nothing had changed. My business was still failing, my marriage was still teetering and my health was still marginal. Yet I felt challenged, excited, motivated, determined, focused, in control and happy.

Why?

Because the events in our lives have no meaning until we give them meaning. I had changed the meaning.

By changing the meaning I changed my beliefs about myself, my life and my future.

And with new beliefs came new feelings.

And with new feelings come new possibilities, new actions.

And all because I used my gift of choice.

Hugh was right. *This is God's greatest gift to us.*

Thank you. Thank you. Thank you.

Chapter 16

"Our thoughts irrevocably determine our destiny," Hugh said, pausing to sip his coffee.

We were sitting in the food court at the airport. Hugh had returned to the hotel and we had both checked out of our rooms. I had driven him to the airport and as he was checking his baggage the agent told us his flight had been delayed for two hours.

"We choose our thoughts, we choose our beliefs, we choose our feelings and we choose our actions. What amazing power we are born with."

"Hugh," I interrupted, "I don't know how to even begin thanking you for being the wonderful friend you have always been. I am so grateful to you for always being there for me. This time you not only saved my life, you gave me a whole new one. I know I can never repay you but if there's ever ..."

He didn't let me finish. "I only did what we promised each other we would do a long time ago. I'm the one who should be thanking you. You gave me an opportunity to share something with my best friend that I have wanted to share for a long time. I knew that this wouldn't happen until you were ready. Your call last week was confirmation to me that you were ready.

"I learned a long time ago never to offer advice until it is asked for. Unsolicited advice causes resentment and is rarely followed anyway. So I prayed for the day when you would ask for my help. Finally my prayers were answered.

"One more thing. It takes immense courage to ask for help and to bare your soul the way you did with me. Most people will go to their graves carrying their burdens deep within themselves for fear of someone seeing their warts. Thank you for placing your trust in me."

I smiled. "I was terrified. I didn't want you, or anyone to know just how many warts I have. But, you know Hugh, that first morning in the hotel room, when I finally shattered that seemingly impenetrable wall I had built around myself and told you everything I didn't want you to know about me, that was the most cathartic moment of my entire life.

There are no words that can accurately describe the feeling of relief I felt at finally getting it out."

"I know," he said gently. "No judgment of us will ever be as painful or cut as deep as the judgment we place on ourselves."

He picked up his carry-on and stood up. "There is a way you can thank me. In fact there are two ways.

"The first is for you to have a life of wonder and joy. You now know how to make that happen, so make God proud. Use the great gift he gave you. Walk the walk. Become the living embodiment of everything you learned this week.

"The second is to consider it your new mission in life to share this wonderful knowledge with as many people as possible. As people who know you begin to notice how you have changed, tell them your story. Every chance you get, pass this on. Write articles, start a blog, give seminars, write a book. Grab any and every opportunity to let as many people as possible in on this magnificent secret.

"Use your great gift of choice to choose a magnificent life."

Hugh hugged me, turned and stood in line to go through security. I watched him disappear and headed back to my car. As I was walking through the concourse I glanced up at the electronic departures board and saw that Hugh's flight had been delayed an additional two hours.

I chuckled to myself. Hugh is an extremely outgoing and gregarious soul. There was no possible way for him to sit in a crowded departures lounge for two hours without making at least one new friend. Some poor, unsuspecting soul was about to have a life changing encounter.

Epilogue:

Thursday December 24

What a difference a short time makes.

That was about nine months ago. Actually, forty-one weeks to be precise. Tonight is Christmas Eve, a magical night for many, and I can't think of a better time to continue my story.

Just thinking about everything that has happened since Hugh boarded that plane leaves me quite breathless.

I had gone home and stayed there for the next four days thinking and planning.

I began with a wish list of anything and everything I could think of and then examined each wish to ensure that it passed the prize and reason test.

I quickly realized that "it would be nice" does not constitute a compelling reason for wanting a prize and I was surprised by how many of those wishes fell off the initial list for lack of a stronger reason than that.

I set goals for myself in many different areas of my life. I set goals around my family, goals for my health and fitness, goals for my business, my relationships and my personal and spiritual development.

I faithfully stayed with the process Hugh had taught me and defined, refined and massaged each goal until I could feel the inevitability of its successful realization.

During this time I was already achieving success in one of my personal development goals; I was taking regular breaks to focus on my affirmathon for fifteen minute periods and the feelings of confidence, certainty and happiness I experienced each time served as confirmation of how essential and powerful this was.

I just knew that even after a few days of 'affirmathoning' I had established a new habit that would remain with me for the rest of my life.

I was now ready to start a new beginning.

I would love to tell you that every day since then has been spectacularly successful, that I have achieved each of my goals in a manner that exceeded my own expectations and that my life was now free of challenges and I was giddy with joy.

That has not been the case. What has happened though is nothing short of remarkable.

Let me give you a short breakdown of how my life has changed since then.

I am significantly lighter than I was the day Hugh boarded the plane to fly home.

Not only am I lighter, I am far healthier as the new habits I have formed include regular workouts as well as healthier nutrition.

The good feelings that came with this success have raised my confidence levels to heights I had never previously imagined possible.

It's amazing what happens when we use our magnificent gift of choice to choose a healthy and energizing lifestyle rather than one that leaves us tired, achy and dispirited.

My marriage has become what I had always dreamed a marriage to be. I have become a far more loving and attentive husband and the rewards are gratifying beyond description.

It's amazing what happens when we use our magnificent gift of choice to choose to be present rather than distant.

The growth in my personal development has filled me with uncontained excitement. I spend at least one hour each day reading and learning.

I have read books on theology, spirituality, enlightenment, human behavior, business, art, biographies, science and so much more that I have come to feel like a sponge, soaking up everything in its presence and always wanting more.

Reading is such a gift that I have become almost evangelical in encouraging everyone I meet to read as if their lives depended on it.

It's amazing what happens when we use our magnificent gift of choice to choose to learn and grow rather than to remain where we are and stagnate.

My business has changed direction by one hundred and eighty degrees. Hugh had told me that one of the ways I could thank him for being there with his life-changing messages when I needed them most was to spread the message of God's gift of choice with as many people as possible.

So I did. I began writing a blog the very first day after I had completed all my goal setting. I publish a new blog every few days and am constantly amazed and delighted by the comments posted on the blog by readers writing to say how understanding the gift of choice has changed their lives.

Interestingly, each time I sit down to write a new blog the words seem to flow off my fingertips onto the screen and yet prior to those few days with Hugh, I was so convinced that I had no writing skills I had never written anything. My fear of writing had been so huge that I had frequently walked away from potential business when a prospective client had asked me to submit a proposal.

I began offering workshops on 'God's Greatest Gift' to anyone interested in attending and these weekly events are now sold-out months in advance.

To my surprise I have learned that I enjoy being in front of an audience whereas, before Hugh, my fear of public speaking would have prevented me from leading a group in silent prayer.

I am even thinking of writing a book on the gift of choice, although I am still a little hesitant to commit to a project of that magnitude.

Interestingly, the more I shared with others, the more my business began to turn itself around. I soon realized that if my intent in going to work was to make money, my struggle would never go away. As soon as my intent changed to give my clients what they wanted, my business began to prosper.

It's amazing what happens when we use our magnificent gift of choice to choose to be providers of service and deliverers of value rather than to focus on personal financial gain.

But by far, the single biggest change has been in me. As I think back to the me who called Hugh and asked for help just a few short months ago I struggle to reconcile that me to the me of today. I can barely recognize that old me.

Everything within me has changed. I wake each morning with the positive expectation that something wonderful is going to happen; and it usually does.

My former practice of rapid and critical judgment of others has almost disappeared as I have learned that most of my criticism stemmed from me seeing traits in others that I despised in myself.

As I have come to love who I am, that inner critical voice is slowly fading away.

My stress levels that used to produce thoughts of suicide in my head have been replaced by calm perspective as I have learned to place new and empowering meaning on events in my life. I now fully understand and live the truth behind Hugh's lesson that while we cannot always control what happens in our lives, we can and do always choose its impact on us.

I feel younger, lighter and more relaxed and while I am, at best, only ten percent of the way up the hill today, I know that tomorrow I'll be a little closer to the top and the day after, even closer.

It's a great feeling.

I have spent a lot of time reflecting on all that has happened to cause all these wonderful changes in my life.

Hugh taught me the importance of overpowering the negative thinking 'muscle' I had developed over many years and make it a priority to take at least four 'me' breaks every single day to instill in myself the feelings of profound gratitude I have for all that my life has given me and to continually reinforce those beliefs and feeling of self-love, confidence, ability, health, intelligence and all those others I have chosen to define the new me.

They sure beat the old ones.

Hugh also taught me how to plan; how to set goals. Understanding the importance of knowing my prize and appreciating what reaching my goals will do for me was crucial in leading me to recognize what my goals needed to be.

And focusing on my reasons, those things that would keep me pointed in the direction of my goals had, indeed, been life-changing.

And finally, identifying those Directional Activities, those few but essential things that I need to do repeatedly and that will move me closer to my goal each time has played a vital role in keeping me on track and in preventing me from deluding myself by doing things that are, perhaps, more comfortable but will not move me any closer to my goal. This has helped me enormously by constantly reminding me that if I don't do those things, I cannot win my prize regardless of how good I feel.

Putting these lessons from Hugh into practice has required a lot of effort on my part and will continue to do so for a long time to come.

It has required hard work and commitment to achieve the success I have enjoyed over these past nine months but, interestingly, the catalyst to all this change, the thing that made this gigantic leap possible, required no work at all.

It all began the moment Hugh told me about the greatest of all gifts we receive from God, the amazing gift of choice.

All the incredible changes in my life that I have just told you about began in that instant. As soon as I 'got' it I used it. I used my God given gift of choice to choose a new life.

From there I developed new beliefs and the rest, as they say, is now history.

The point I'm trying to make is this; massive, lasting change in our lives begins as soon as we take the first simple step.

Make a new choice.

No effort required.

About the Author

Rael Kalley has been in the coaching, consulting and training business for more than twenty-five years.

Born in South Africa, Rael moved to Canada in 1977. He soon developed his passion for helping others identify their goals and create meaningful activities to achieve them. As his success continued, Rael developed a process to ensure consistent results for himself and his clients.

He is the creator of On Course, a goal setting and planning model that helps his clients shape their futures and reach their potential.

Rael is the president and CEO of Strategic Pathways Inc., a full service leadership consulting company which he founded in 1995.

Rael lives in Calgary, Alberta with his wife.

Contact us

If you would like Rael to present a workshop to your organization or if you would like more information on the coaching, and consulting services offered by Rael Kalley and Strategic Pathways please visit our websites at **www.strategicpathways.net** or **www.raelkalley.com**

You can also call Rael toll-free at 1-888-232-1136 or send an email to rael@raelkalley.com.

Please help me reach my goal

I write a blog which I post every Saturday. You can find my blog by visiting **www.raelkalley.com** and clicking on the link.

The blog is intended to be light-hearted and humorous with a serious message that follows the philosophy that Hugh shared with Earl in this book.

I have a goal of reaching 100,000 email subscribers. Please help me by subscribing to my blog and passing it along to your friends.

Thank you,

Rael Kalley

Acknowledgements

My life has been a blessed with the gift of wonderful friendships.

Despite my best efforts to make poor choices and even poorer mistakes my friends have remained my friends and while I m sure many of them have shaken their heads in bewilderment, they have never judged me harshly and have unconditionally given me their friendship.

The list includes, but is, by no means, limited to, Al, Alan, Ali, Bill, Bob, Brenda, Brian, Bruce, Cameron, Cathy, Cindy, David, Deb, Debbie, Doug, Frank, Gabe, Gary, Garth, Gerald, Gerry, Gill, Greg, Gregg, Howard, Ivan, Jerry, Joan, Jeff, Jill, Jim, John, Karen, Katherine, Ken, Leisa, Linda, Lisa, Mel, Melanie, Michael, Michelle, Mike, Norm, Paul, Phil, Richard, Rick, Sanjay, Sodi, Terry, Tony, Vince, Vicki, William.

There is one more and she is the one to whom my debt of gratitude can never be repaid.

My beautiful wife, Gimalle, has, for the past fourteen years, been the rock in my life upon whom I have leaned for support, inspiration, encouragement, motivation and just plain, old fashioned, from the heart, friendship.

To all of you, **thank you**.